I Can Find Letter Sounds

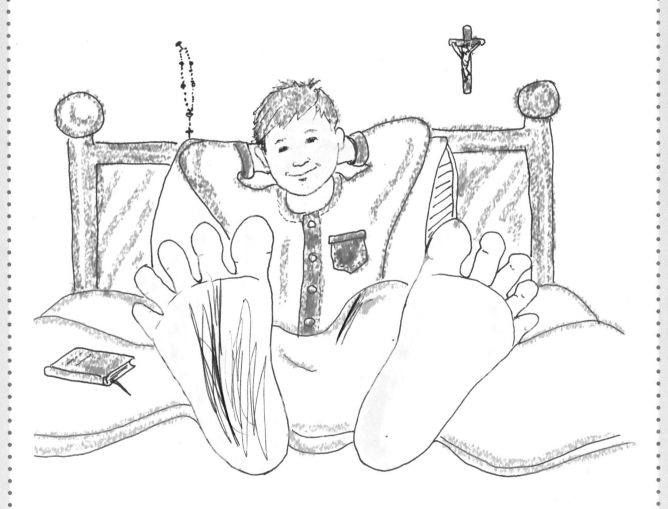

Nancy Nicholson

A M
D G

For Little Folks

Dedicated to
the Child Jesus:
may He reign in hearts big and small.

Image Credits:
Illustrated by Nancy Nicholson. Complete image credits can be found on page 93.

ISBN: 978-0-9836832-9-2

Printed by Transcontinental Interglobe
Beauceville, Qc, Canada
October 2023

Catholic Heritage Curricula
1-800-490-7713 *www.chcweb.com*

Table of Contents

Introduction

This "ready for learning" pre-writing workbook reinforces the preschool child's study of letter shapes and sounds through multi-sensory learning activities. Multisensory learning activities spark interest and improve retention by engaging as many senses as possible in an active, hands-on fashion.

Follow the steps below to teach each letter. In *CHC Lesson Plans for Preschool*, the recommended schedule is to complete one step per day, four days a week. At this pace, one letter will be covered each week.

Step 1: Introduce and Color the Letter

On the left-hand page of each lesson, show your child the uppercase and lowercase forms of the featured letter. Introduce the letter by stressing that it has a **name** and a **sound**, which generally differs from its name. For example, "The name of this letter is A; it says *aaaaaaa* as in *aaaapplesauce*. See the drawing of applesauce in the jar? See the little apples at the top of the page? They start with the sound of A too: *aaaaapple*." Instruct the child to color the pictures and letters on both pages of the lesson.

> It is very important to introduce only short vowel sounds at this age; refer to the Alphabet Sounds List on page 4.

Step 2: Make Alphabet Card

Involve the child in creating a decorated alphabet card for the featured letter, using one of the options below. Encourage the child to trace over the decorated letter frequently with his finger while repeating its name and sound; this exercise develops both visual and tactile familiarity with the letter. If space allows, you may wish to post the alphabet cards on the wall at the child's level so he can trace the letters as he recites his ABCs.

- Write the upper- and lowercase forms of the featured letter in large print on an 8½" x 11" piece of cardstock. Trace the letters with glue, then cover each letter with brightly colored strands of string or yarn, glitter, cake decorating sprinkles, or colored rice or salt. (Either salt or dry rice can be colored by shaking them with a few drops of food coloring in a small jar. Allow the salt/rice to dry overnight before using.) Shake off excess matter and allow glue to dry.

- Write the upper- and lowercase forms of the featured letter in large print on an 8½" x 11" piece of cardstock. Trace the letters with an item beginning with that letter sound. For example, the letter "A" can be traced with apple stickers, "B" with dry beans, "C" with coffee grounds, and so on. Allow child to decorate the area around the letter with pictures and stickers of things that begin with that letter sound. (Ideas for this option can be found in *CHC Lesson Plans for Preschool*.)

> Anytime your child gets "fidgety," invite him to play "Skip to My ABCs" or another of the Active Learning Games detailed on pages 5–8.

Step 3: Find the Letter Sound

On the right-hand page of each lesson, read the devotional sentence at the top of the page. Point to the sentence and demonstrate that the first word begins with the featured letter. For example, "Do you see the letter A at the beginning of this word? Listen for the sound of A when I read, '*Aaaask* Jesus to bless you today.'"

Direct the child to find things around the house that start with the featured letter sound. A list of ideas is included in each lesson. Say, "Now you are going to find some things that start with the sound of A. These are some things that start with *aaaaa*. [Read the list of **A** words to your child, emphasizing the short vowel sound of **A**: *aaanimal, aaaapplesauce, aaaapple, aaants*.] Can you find any of these things in our house?" As the child finds things around the house, repeat their names together, emphasizing the beginning sound of each.

Step 4: Cut and Paste

Now have the child search through the image bank on pages 79–87 of this workbook to find and cut out pictures of things that start with the featured letter sound. Say, "Can you find pictures of things that start with the sound of A? Find all the things that start with *aaaaa*." There are three pictures in the image bank for each letter, which correspond to the last three items on the checklist.

Instruct the child to paste the three pictures he has found in the "I Can Find" box in his workbook. The fourth space in the "I Can Find" box is reserved for the child to draw something that starts with the featured letter sound.

Encourage your child at every opportunity to find things that begin with letter sounds that he is currently studying. Allow him to look at canned and boxed goods, at home and as you are grocery shopping, to find and imitate letter sounds. Or give your child an old newspaper and a crayon, point to the large-lettered headlines and instruct him to circle every B or whatever letter he may be learning that day.

The child may also enjoy looking for pictures in unwanted magazines, catalogs, or sale ads. Food labels from cans and boxes are another resource. The pictures can be cut out and saved in an envelope marked with the featured letter. A good way to review letters is to empty two or three envelopes of pictures onto his workspace and ask him to sort the pictures back into their proper envelopes.

In some cases the child may identify a picture from the image bank differently than expected. For instance, he may say "boy" instead of "jump rope" for the image showing a boy jumping rope. Simply praise the child and ask him to find something else in the image that starts with the "J as in juh" letter sound that you are looking for. However, do correct him if he misidentifies the beginning sound of an object. Say, "No, *pig* starts with a different sound. It starts with *puh*, not *buh*. Can you hear the difference? *Buh, puh.* Let's look for a picture that starts with *buh*."

Alphabet Sounds List

Exaggerating the sound of each letter will help the child identify its sound within the context of words. Only short vowel sounds are provided at this level to lessen confusion and facilitate learning.

Aa as in aaa-applesauce

Bb as in "buh" banana and button

Cc as in "kuh" carrot and can

Dd as in "duh" door and dress

Ee as in eeh-elephant and eh-egg

Ff as in "ffff" flower and football

Gg as in "guh" glove

Hh as in "huh" hamburger and heart

Ii as in iii-insect

Jj as in "juh-juh" Jesus

Kk as in "kuh" key and kitten

Ll as in llll-lollipop

Mm as in mmm-Mary

Nn as in nnn-nut

Oo as in "o"-ostrich and olive

Pp as in "puh" pitcher and pear

Qq as in "kwuh" quilt and quick

Rr as in rrrr-radish

Ss as in ssss-sandwich and sock

Tt as in "tuh" toes and trees

Uu as in "uuuh" up and umbrella

Vv as in "vuh" vacuum and vase

Ww as in "wuh" watermelon and whistle

Xx as in extra and fox*

Yy as in "yuh" yellow and yolks

Zz as in zzz-zebra and zoo

*Point out that we hear the "x" sound at the **end** of "fox," instead of at the beginning.*

Active Learning Games

These active games require 26 sheets of cardstock paper, about 8½" x 11" each. With a marker, print upper- and lowercase letters—Aa, Bb, Cc, and so on—one letter to each sheet, and as large as the sheet allows.

It is best to wait to begin these games until after the child has mastered at least the first few letters of the alphabet.

Skip to My ABCs!

Beginner's Level
A game for the beginner, who can't yet identify any letters.

Make a pile of the letter sheets in alphabetical order, with A on top and Z on the bottom. Set the pile on one side of the room. (The objective is to make a sequential line of the ABCs across the room from the pile.)

The child takes the first sheet, singing, "Skip, skip, skip to my A; Skip, skip, skip to my A..." (to the tune of "Skip to My Lou"), while skipping across the room to place the first card.

The child returns for the second sheet, singing, "Skip, skip, skip to my B..." etc. and skips across the room to place the second card. Continue until all the letter sheets have been placed in order.

When all the numbers are in order, say the alphabet together while pointing to each letter. Congratulate the child for a job well done.

"Simon Says" ABC Path

Beginner's Level

Lay the letter sheets on the floor in a meandering path, leaving about 12 inches between letter sheets.

The person taking the role of Simon commands the player: "Simon says, step over the letter A." The child answers "A," and steps over the letter A.

Simon commands the player: "Simon says, pat your head" (or a similar command). The child answers, "Pat my head," and pats his head.

Simon commands the player: "Simon says, step over the letter B." The child answers, "B," and steps over the letter B.

Simon commands the player, "Step over the letter C." The child answers, "C," but does not step over the letter because the command isn't preceded by "Simon says." (If the child steps anyway, say "Simon caught you!" and the child steps back one letter.)

Continue play in this manner, issuing various commands to step over letters, raise hands, rub tummies, hop on one foot, etc., some commands preceded by "Simon says" and some commands without.

When the player reaches the letter "Z," he takes Simon's place and the previous Simon becomes the player.

If the child is just beginning to learn the alphabet, set out only the first twelve letter sheets. When the child has learned the first twelve letters, add the next twelve letters to the path.

Simple Match-Up

Beginner's Level

Also needed: Alphabet flashcards

Lay all the 8½" x 11" letter sheets in a line on the floor, in alphabetical order.

Give the child the "A" flashcard, identify the letter for him, and instruct him to find the matching 8½" x 11" letter sheet. When he finds the "match," say, "Good job! Yes, that's the 'A.'" The child lays the matching flashcard on the larger version and returns for the second card.

Independent variation: Give the child the flashcards and instruct him to find the matching cards, laying the smaller flashcards on top of the larger letter sheets as he finds "matches." This game will not teach the names of the letters, but will help the child begin to differentiate between letters.

ABC Criss-Cross

Intermediate Level

For this game, the child needs to be able to identify at least six of the first twelve letters of the alphabet.

Also needed: Alphabet flashcards

Begin with the first twelve letters of the alphabet only.

In random order, lay out six of the 8½" x 11" letter sheets on one side of the room and six of the sheets on the other side.

Call out the first letter: "A!" The child races to stand in front of the letter sheet. (If the child needs a "prompt," hold up the matching flashcard and say, "Remember that 'A' looks like this.")

Call out "B!" The child rushes to locate and stand in front of the letter sheet.

Continue to call out the letters until the child has found the last letter. When the child is able to identify the first twelve letters of the alphabet, add three more.

This game may be timed with a kitchen timer to encourage the child to "beat the buzzer."

Warm C, Cold C

Intermediate Level

Begin with the first twelve 8½" x 11" letter sheets only.

From these twelve letter sheets, separate the letters that the child can identify from those that he cannot identify. Set aside the letter sheets that he cannot identify.

Begin by laying the letters A and B on the floor against one wall, even if the child cannot identify them. Then lay out, in alphabetical order, the remainder of the letters that the child can identify, leaving spaces to place missing letters.

Adult sits across the room, holding the letter sheets that the child cannot identify. The child takes the first sheet from the adult (for example, "C"). The adult tells the child the name of the letter; the child repeats "C," and is sent to find the correct empty space for the letter sheet in his hand.

The adult "coaches" by saying "Warm 'C,' warmer 'C'!" as the child nears the correct space and "Cold 'C,' colder 'C'!" if the child moves away from the correct space. When the child places the letter sheet in the correct spot, begin again with the next letter to be placed. When several sheets have been placed, encourage the child to use the ABC song for clues as to which card comes next.

Add three more letters to the game as the child masters the first twelve letters.

I Can Find Letter Sounds

Aa Aa Aa

I can find things that start with the sound of A a.

- ☐ animal
- ☐ applesauce
- ☐ apple
- ☐ ants
- ☐ alligator

I Can Find...

See pages 79–87.

To the Parent:

When introducing the upper- and lowercase forms of **A** at the top of page 10, point out that lowercase **A** can be written two ways: ɑ or **a**.

Remember to teach only the short vowel sound of **A**, as heard in the word *applesauce* (see Alphabet Sounds List, pg. 4).

B   b

Bb Bb

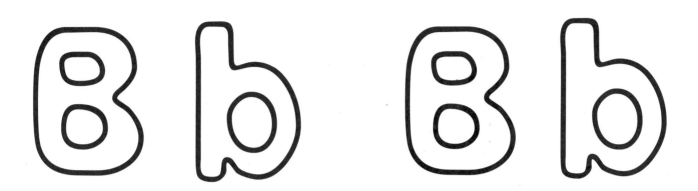

I can find things that start with the sound of B b.

- ☐ banana
- ☐ bowl
- ☐ baby
- ☐ buttons
- ☐ bat
- ☐ ball
- ☐ books
- ☐ bread
- ☐ bathtub
- ☐ Bible
- ☐ bird
- ☐ boy

I Can Find...

To the Parent:

The child may cut and paste a photo of *brother* or *baby* in the fourth "I Can Find" box.

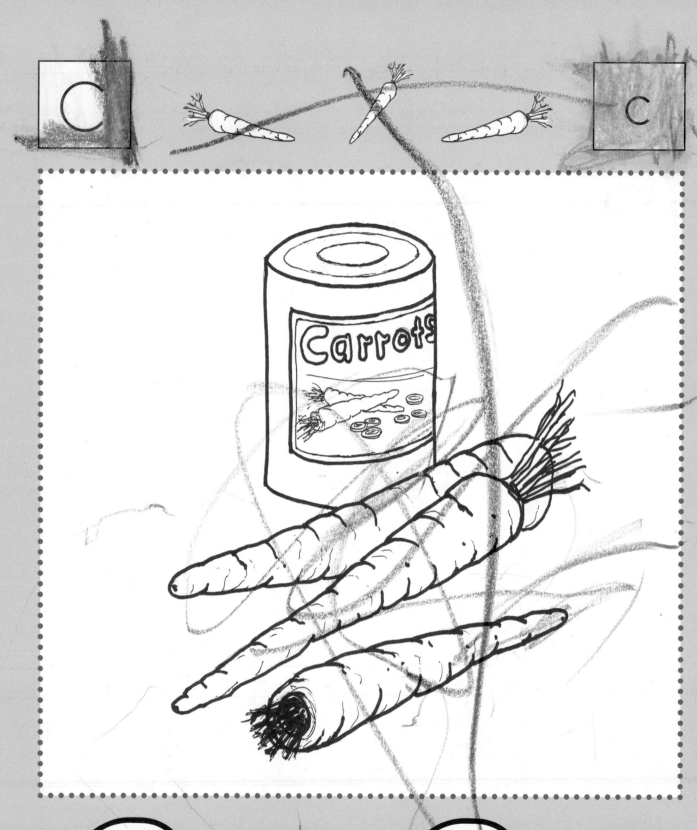

C C C C

14

Come, Jesus, into my heart.

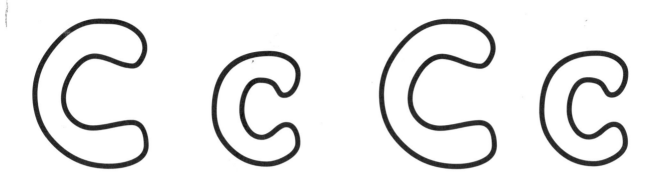

I can find things that start with the sound of C c.

- ☐ cans
- ☐ comb
- ☐ carrot
- ☐ crucifix
- ☐ colors
- ☐ cup
- ☐ candy
- ☐ corn
- ☐ cow
- ☐ crown
- ☐ cupcake

I Can Find...

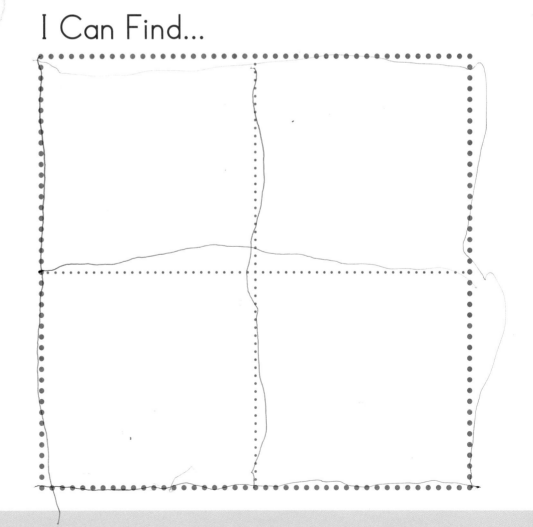

D    d

Dd Dd

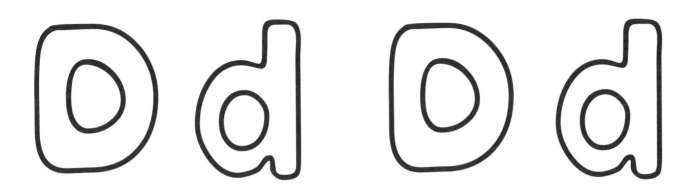

I can find things that start with the sound of D d.

☐ dress
☐ door
☐ doll
☐ dog
☐ donut
☐ duck

I Can Find...

To the Parent:

The child may cut and paste a photo of *Dad* in the "I Can Find" box.

17

E   e

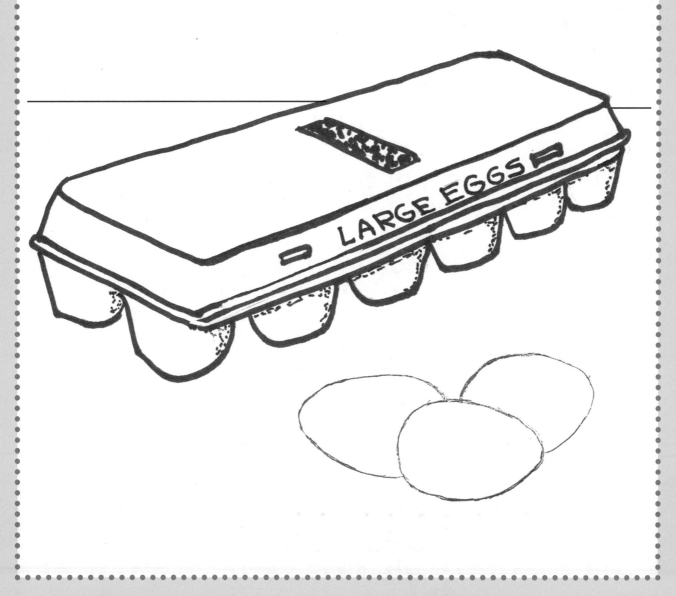

LARGE EGGS

Ɛe Ɛe

ENTER

EXIT

"Enter and Exit" Game: Instead of searching for things that start with the sound of E, ask the child to color and cut out the ENTER and EXIT signs above. Players pick one person to be the "mover." A small object such as a ping pong ball or small block is given to the "mover." The "mover" holds up the EXIT sign, and all players leave to another room. The "mover" places the object in sight, such as on the back of a sofa or on a bookshelf. He then goes to the room where the other players are waiting and holds up the "ENTER" sign. Players enter the room with the "moved" object. First person to spot the object becomes the next "mover" to place the object in a new place, etc.

Remember to teach only the short vowel sound of **E**, as heard in the word *elephant* (see Alphabet Sounds List, pg. 4).

This page intentionally left blank.

I can match letter sounds.

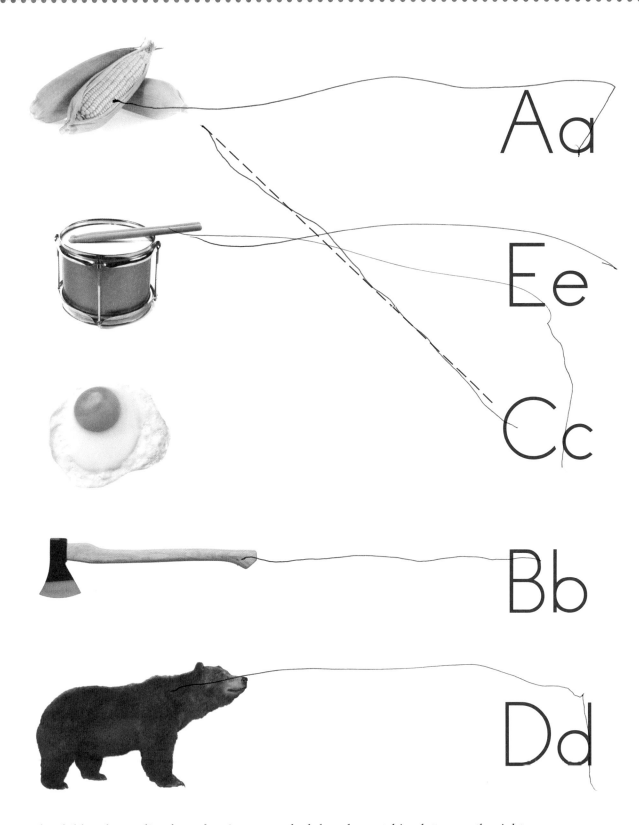

Instruct the child to draw a line from the pictures on the left to the matching letters on the right.

F   f

F f F f

I can find things that start with the sound of F f.

- ☐ fork
- ☐ flowers
- ☐ flowerpot
- ☐ fingers
- ☐ faucet
- ☐ football
- ☐ fish
- ☐ frog
- ☐ flag
- ☐ fox

To the Parent:

The child may cut and paste a photo of a *friend* in the "I Can Find" box.

I Can Find...

23

Lowercase **G** can be written two ways.

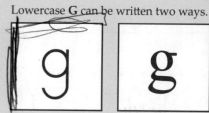

G g g

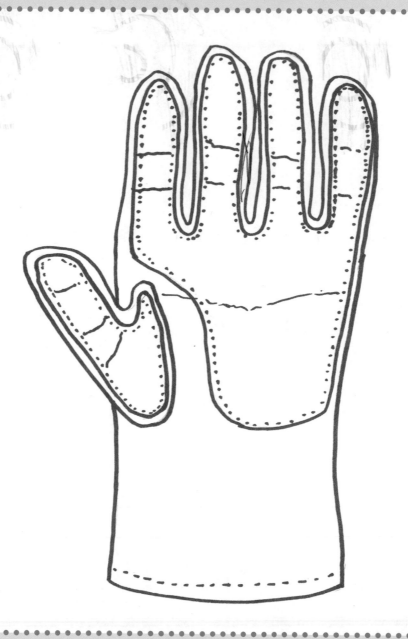

Gg Gg

24

G g G g

I can find things that start with the sound of G g.

- ☐ gum
- ☐ gift
- ☐ girl
- ☐ grapes
- ☐ glasses
- ☐ gloves

I Can Find...

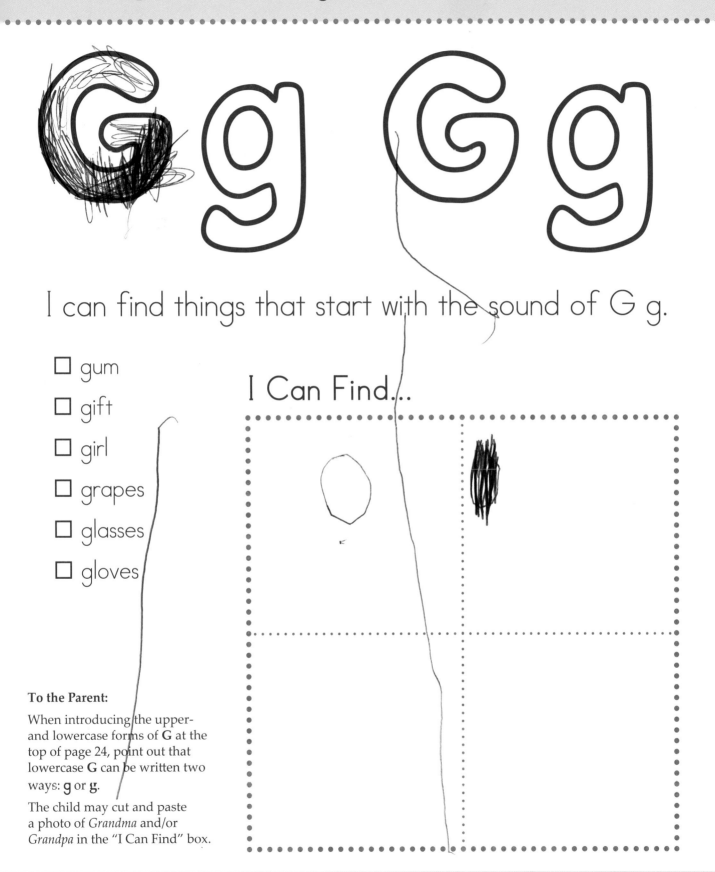

To the Parent:

When introducing the upper- and lowercase forms of **G** at the top of page 24, point out that lowercase **G** can be written two ways: **g** or **g**.

The child may cut and paste a photo of *Grandma* and/or *Grandpa* in the "I Can Find" box.

H

h

Hh Hh

Hh Hh

I can find things that start with the sound of H h.

- ☐ hamburger
- ☐ hot dog
- ☐ hand
- ☐ hammer
- ☐ hat
- ☐ horse
- ☐ heart
- ☐ house

I Can Find...

To the Parent:

The child may cut and paste a photo of his *home* in the "I Can Find" box.

I i

Insects!

"In" Game: Instead of searching for things that start with the sound of **I**, instruct the child to color the heart on each "in" card. The heart means "I love you and I prayed for you." Invite the child to cut out the cards and place them *in* family members' drawers, pocket, cup, etc., after praying for them.

Remember to teach only the short vowel sound of **I**, as heard in the word *insect* (see Alphabet Sounds List, pg. 4).

This page intentionally left blank.

I can match letter sounds.

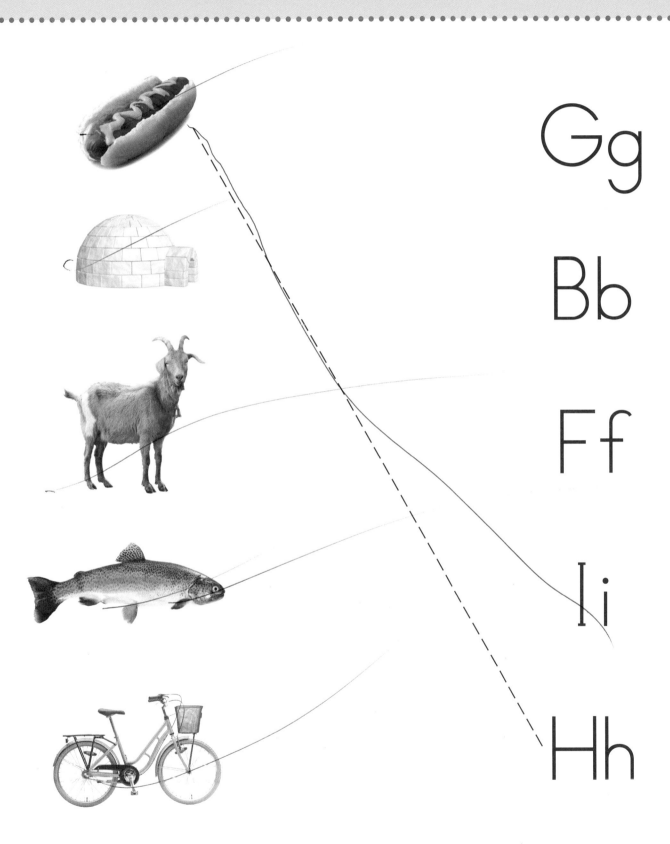

Gg

Bb

Ff

Ii

Hh

Instruct the child to draw a line from the pictures on the left to the matching letters on the right.

Uppercase **J** can be written two ways.

J J j

Jesus made me, Jesus loves me, Jesus cares for me.

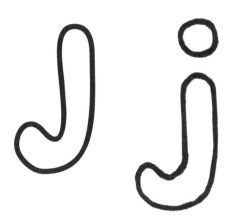 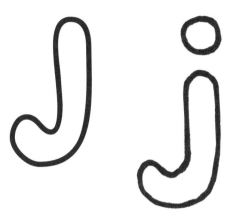

I can find things that start with the sound of J j.
How many pictures of Jesus can you find in your house?

☐ juice

☐ jelly

☐ jar

☐ jump rope

☐ Jesus

☐ jam

I Can Find...

To the Parent:

The child may paste a holy card of *Jesus* and/or *St. Joseph* in the "I Can Find" box.

K   k

K k K k

K k K k

I can find things that start with the sound of K k.

☐ kitten

☐ keys

☐ kettle

☐ kitchen

☐ king

☐ kite

☐ kangaroo

I Can Find...

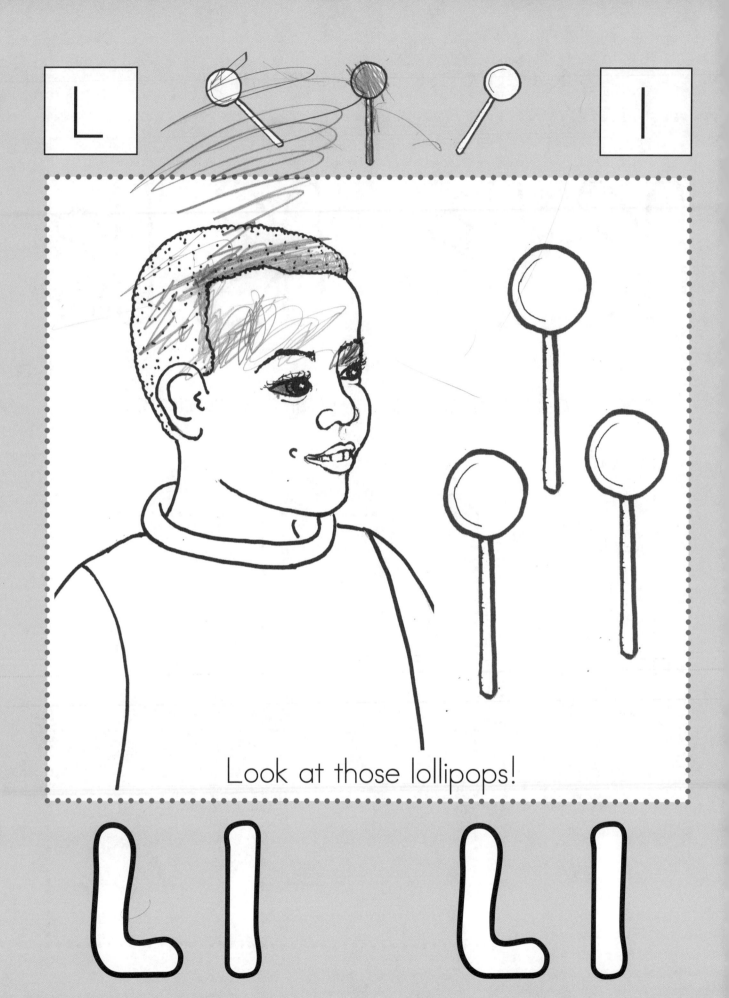

L   l

Look at those lollipops!

I can find things that start with the sound of L l.

☐ leaf

☐ lollipop

☐ lightbulb

☐ lotion

☐ lamp

☐ ladybug

☐ lizard

☐ lion

I Can Find...

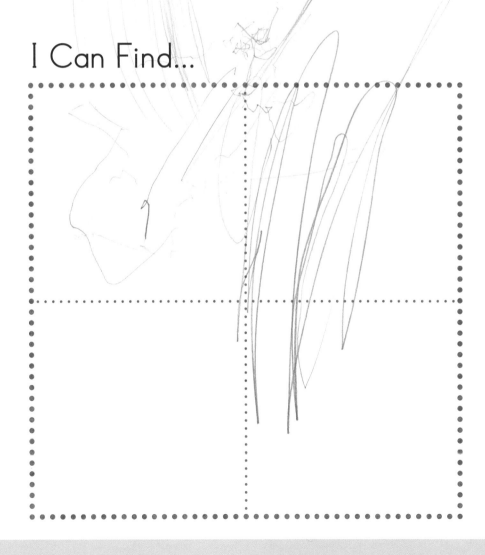

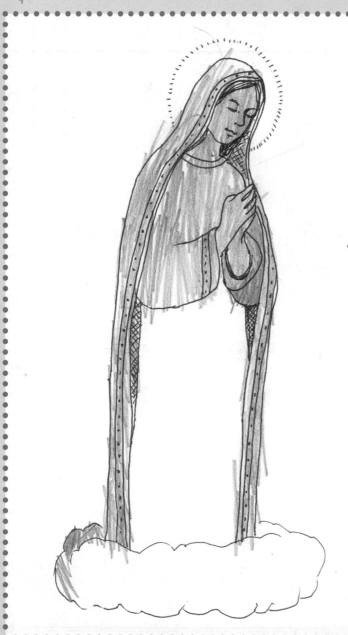

Hail Mary,
full of grace,
the Lord is
with you!

Luke 1:28

Mm Mm

I can find things that start with the sound of M m.

- ☐ medal
- ☐ milk
- ☐ mitten
- ☐ macaroni
- ☐ mushrooms
- ☐ mail
- ☐ marshmallow
- ☐ money
- ☐ Mary
- ☐ mailbox

I Can Find...

To the Parent:

The child may cut and paste a photo of *Mom* and/or *me* in the "I Can Find" box.

N n N n

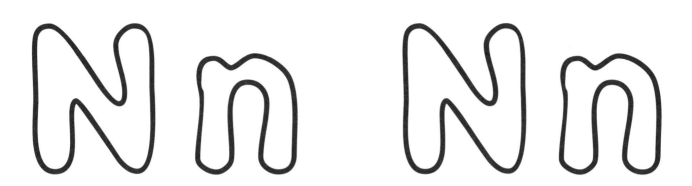

I can find things that start with the sound of N n.

☐ nuts

☐ noodles

☐ nightlight

☐ nest

☐ net

☐ nails

I Can Find...

Ostrich

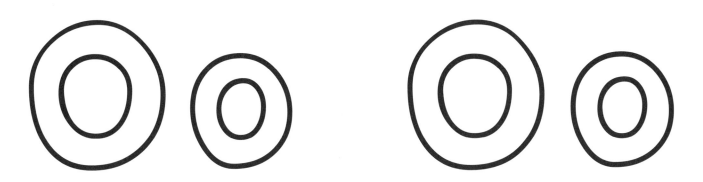
I can find things on top. Circle and color shapes that have an X on top.

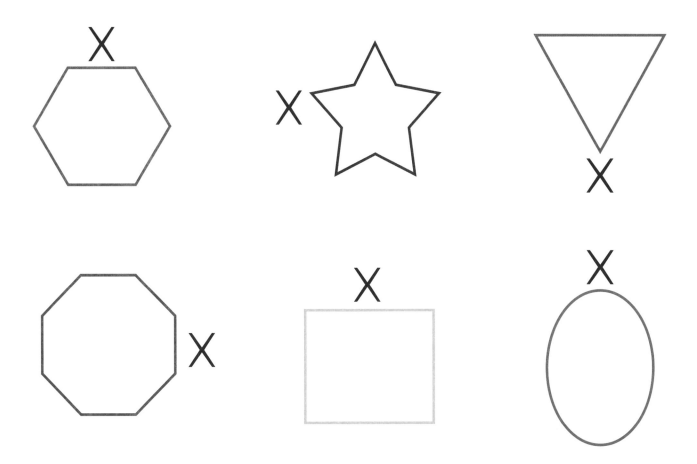

Instead of searching for things that start with the sound of **O**, instruct the child to circle and color only the shapes with Xs on top.

Remember to teach only the short vowel sound of **O**, as heard in the word *ostrich* (see Alphabet Sounds List, pg. 4).

I can match letters.

Instruct the child to draw a line from the uppercase letters to the matching lowercase letters.

I can match letter sounds.

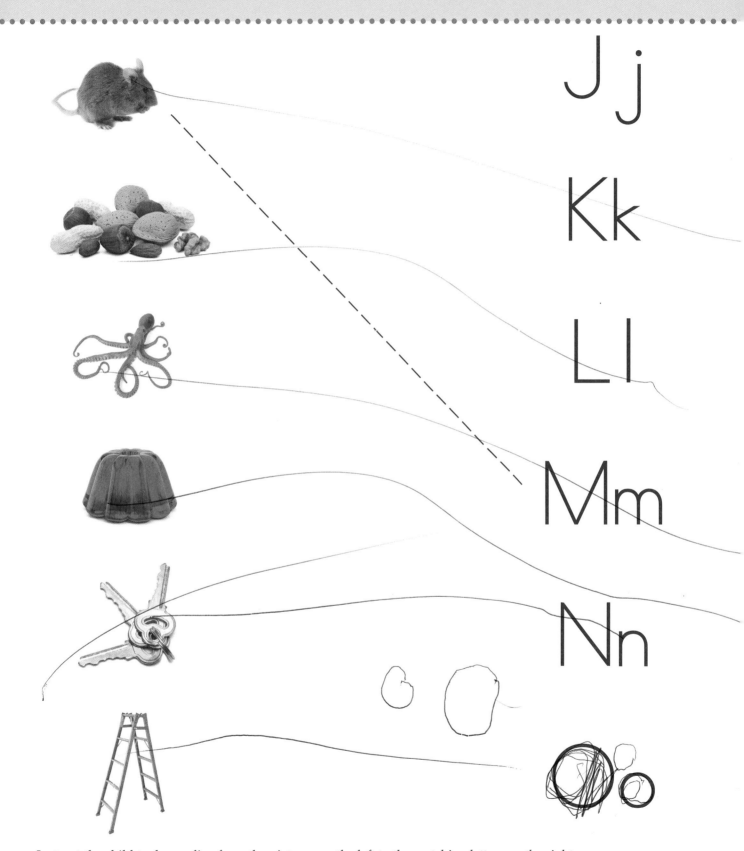

J j

K k

L l

M m

N n

O o

Instruct the child to draw a line from the pictures on the left to the matching letters on the right.

P   p

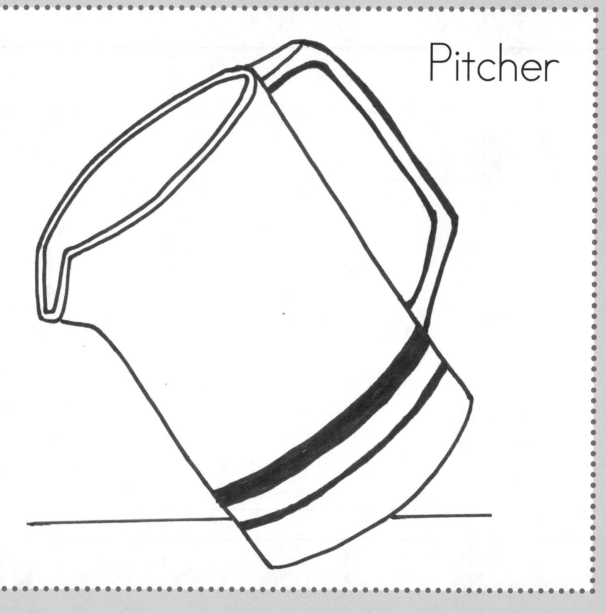

Pitcher

P p P p

46

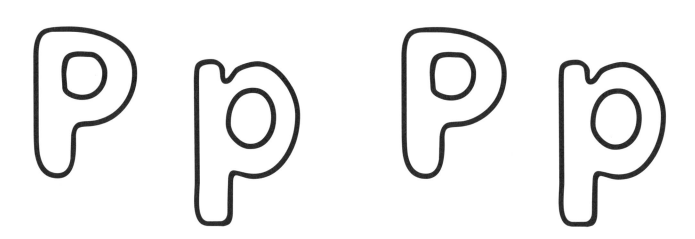

I can find things that start with the sound of P p.

- ☐ pitcher
- ☐ pants
- ☐ pencil
- ☐ paints
- ☐ pan
- ☐ pear
- ☐ pillow
- ☐ pie
- ☐ pizza
- ☐ priest

I Can Find...

To the Parent:

The child may cut and paste a photo of his *pet* in the "I Can Find" box.

Tony says, "Quick! Start the game!"

Q q Q q

QUIT

QUICK

Quit and Quick Game: Instead of searching for things that start with the sound of **Q**, instruct the child to color the QUIT sign red and the QUICK sign green and then cut them out. Establish start and finish points for a "race course," and select one player to be the "traffic director." When the traffic director holds up the green QUICK card, players race for the finish line. At any point, the traffic director may flash the QUIT card and players must freeze in place until the traffic director flashes the QUICK card again. The traffic director continues flashing the QUICK and QUIT cards until a player reaches the finish line. The winner becomes the next traffic director.

This page intentionally left blank.

I can match letter sounds.

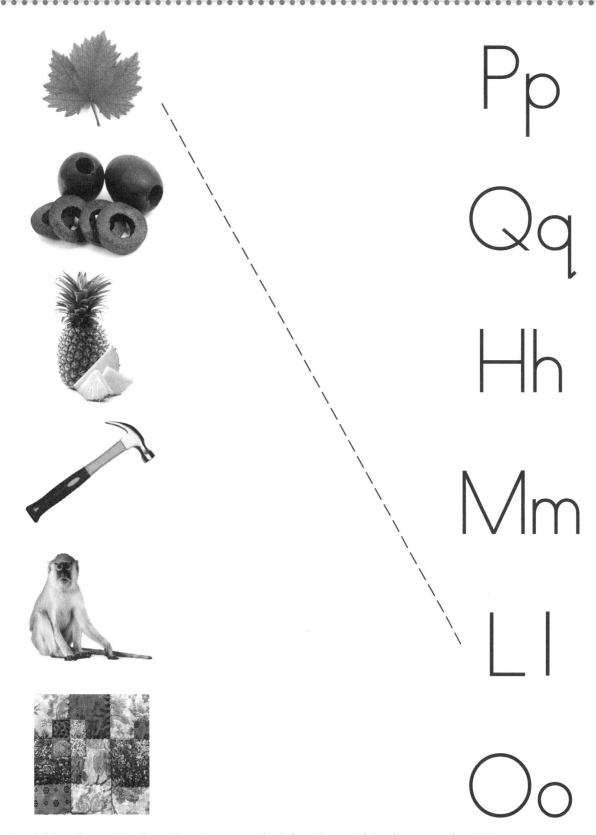

P p

Q q

H h

M m

L l

O o

Instruct the child to draw a line from the pictures on the left to the matching letters on the right.

R    r

R r R r

I can find things that start with the sound of R r.

- ☐ radish
- ☐ radio
- ☐ ring
- ☐ ribbon
- ☐ race car
- ☐ rabbit
- ☐ rake
- ☐ rainbow
- ☐ rosary

I Can Find...

S    s

Ss Ss

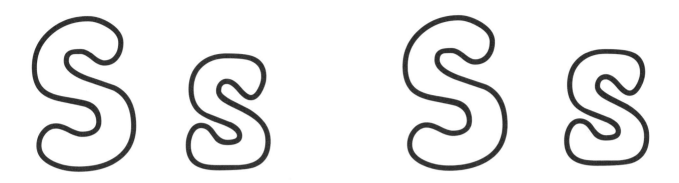

I can find things that start with the sound of S s.

- ☐ socks
- ☐ saltshaker
- ☐ sandwich
- ☐ spoon
- ☐ stool
- ☐ slippers
- ☐ sack
- ☐ slide
- ☐ strawberries
- ☐ snowman

I Can Find...

To the Parent:

The child may cut and paste a photo of *sister* in the "I Can Find" box.

T   t

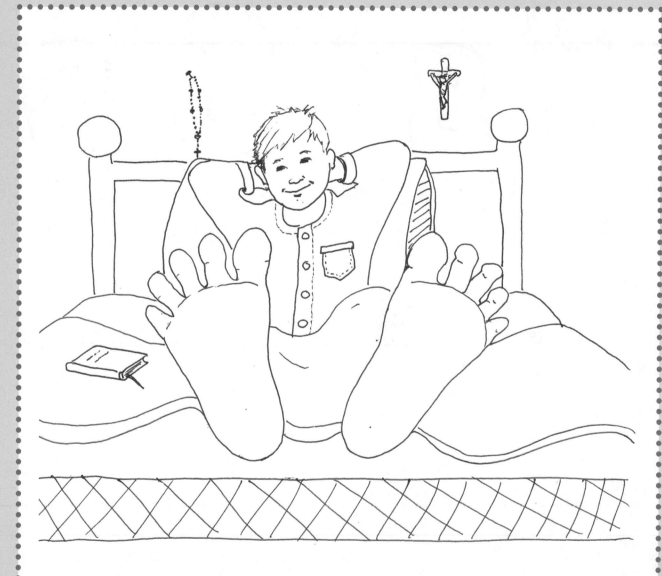

Tony's toes

T t T t

I can find things that start with the sound of T t.

- ☐ toes
- ☐ tissue
- ☐ toothbrush
- ☐ table
- ☐ trike
- ☐ truck
- ☐ teddy bear
- ☐ tape
- ☐ tie
- ☐ tree
- ☐ turtle
- ☐ tabernacle
- ☐ teepee

I Can Find...

What are some things that you might see up in the sky? Draw them in the square below.

Instruct the child to draw and color things he might see *up* in the sky.

I see things that are up.

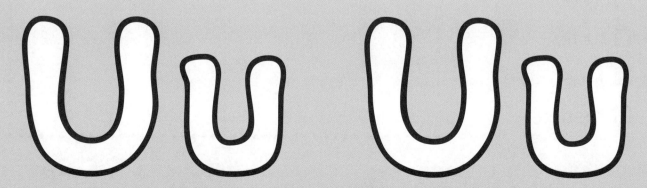

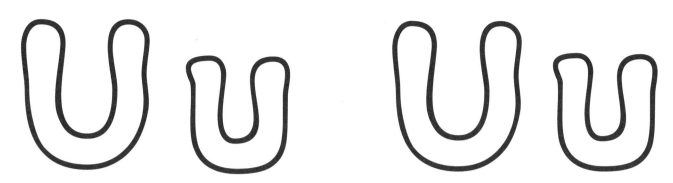

I can find things that are under. Circle and color shapes that have an X underneath.

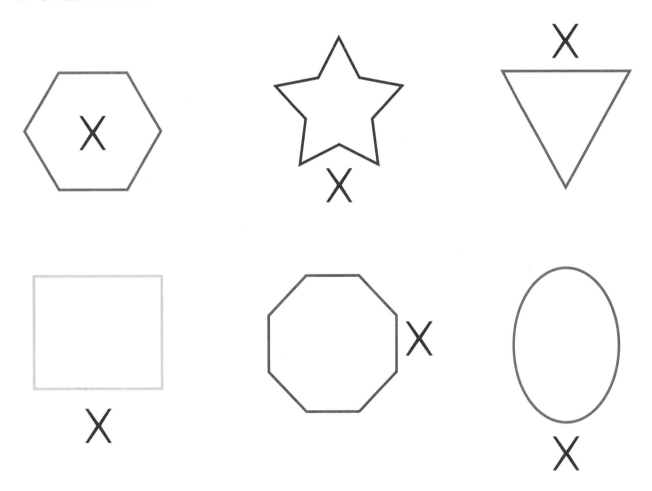

Instruct the child to circle and color only the shapes with Xs underneath.

Remember to teach only the short vowel sound of **U**, as heard in the word *up* (see Alphabet Sounds List, pg. 4).

I can match letters.

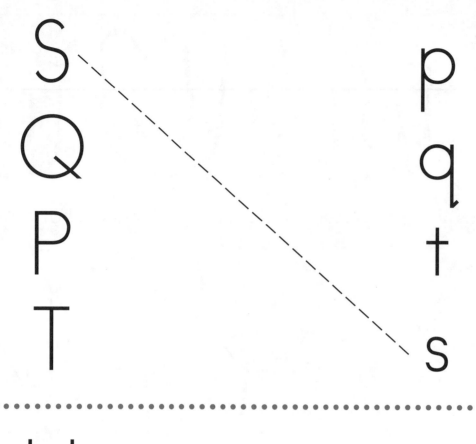

S
Q
P
T

p
q
t
s

U
N
O
R

o
r
u
n

Instruct the child to draw a line from the uppercase letters to the matching lowercase letters.

I can match letter sounds.

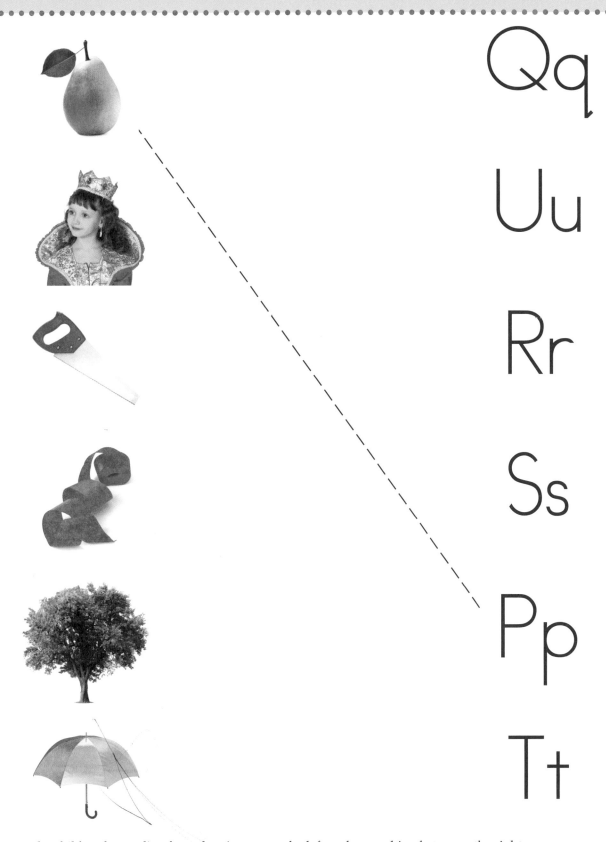

Qq

Uu

Rr

Ss

Pp

Tt

Instruct the child to draw a line from the pictures on the left to the matching letters on the right.

Tony helps vacuum.

V v V v

Visit Jesus in the tabernacle.

I can find things that start with the sound of V v.

☐ vacuum

☐ vest

☐ vinegar

☐ vitamins

☐ violin

☐ van

☐ vase

I Can Find...

Tell the child the story of
St. Veronica and her veil
before asking him to find things
that start with the sound of **V**.

  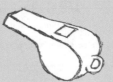

WwWw

Ww Ww

I can find things that start with the sound of W w.

☐ window

☐ water

☐ watch

☐ whistle

☐ washcloth

☐ wagon

☐ worm

☐ watering can

☐ watermelon

I Can Find...

St. Andrew's Cross and Shield

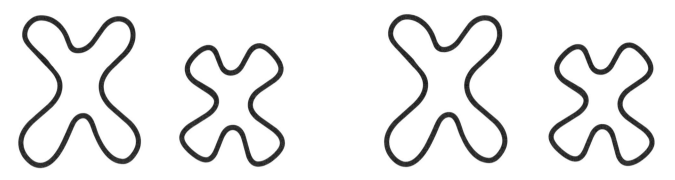

Two hands and two feet need
two mittens and two slippers.
Put an X on the extras.

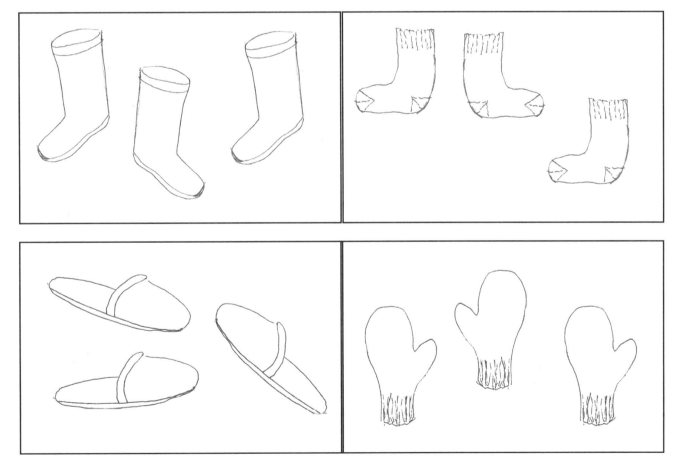

Instruct the child to put an X on the *extra* objects, then color the ones he did not X out.

I can match letters.

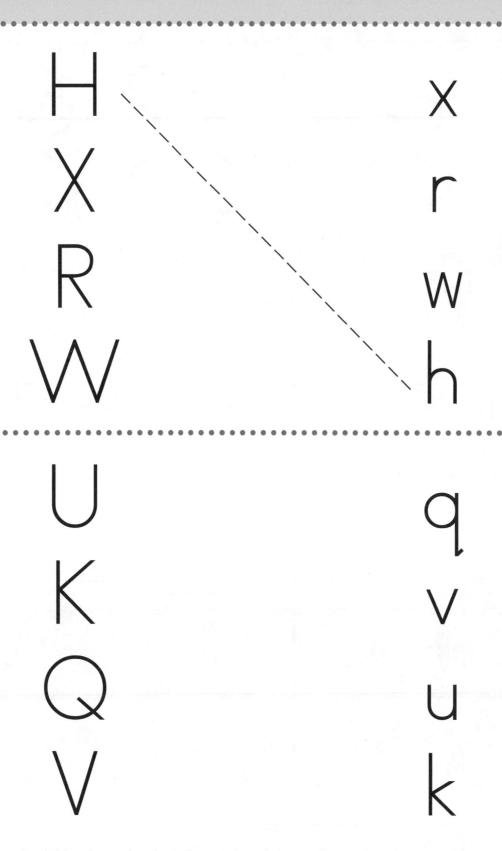

H
X
R
W

U
K
Q
V

x
r
w
h

q
v
u
k

Instruct the child to draw a line from the uppercase letters to the matching lowercase letters.

I can match letter sounds.

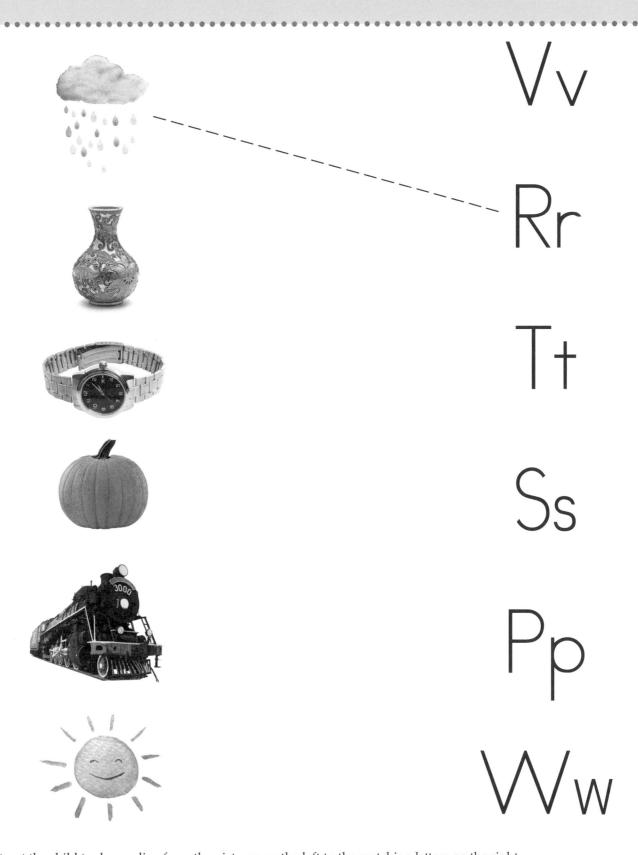

Instruct the child to draw a line from the pictures on the left to the matching letters on the right.

Y

y

Yolks are yellow.

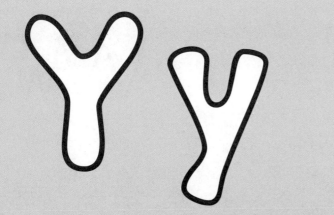

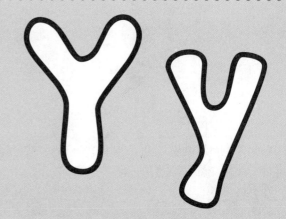

70

You are my very best friend, dear Jesus.

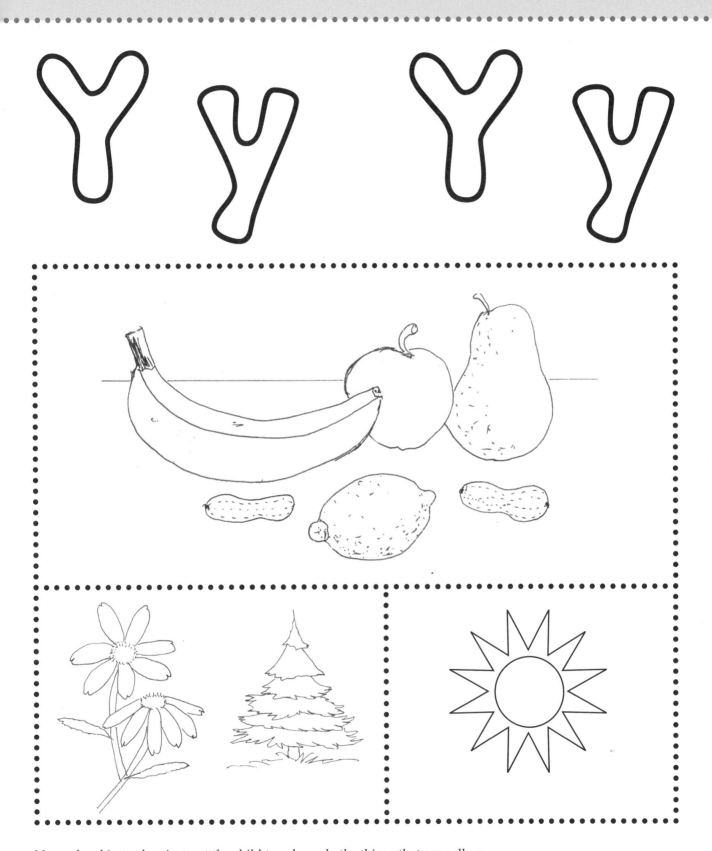

Name the objects, then instruct the child to color only the things that are yellow.

I can match letters.

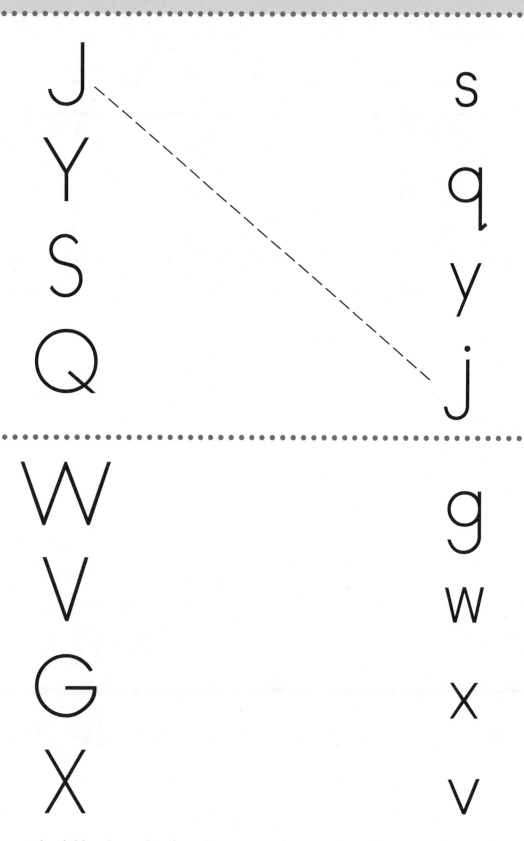

J   s

Y   q

S   y

Q   j

W   g

V   w

G   x

X   v

Instruct the child to draw a line from the uppercase letters to the matching lowercase letters.

I can match letter sounds.

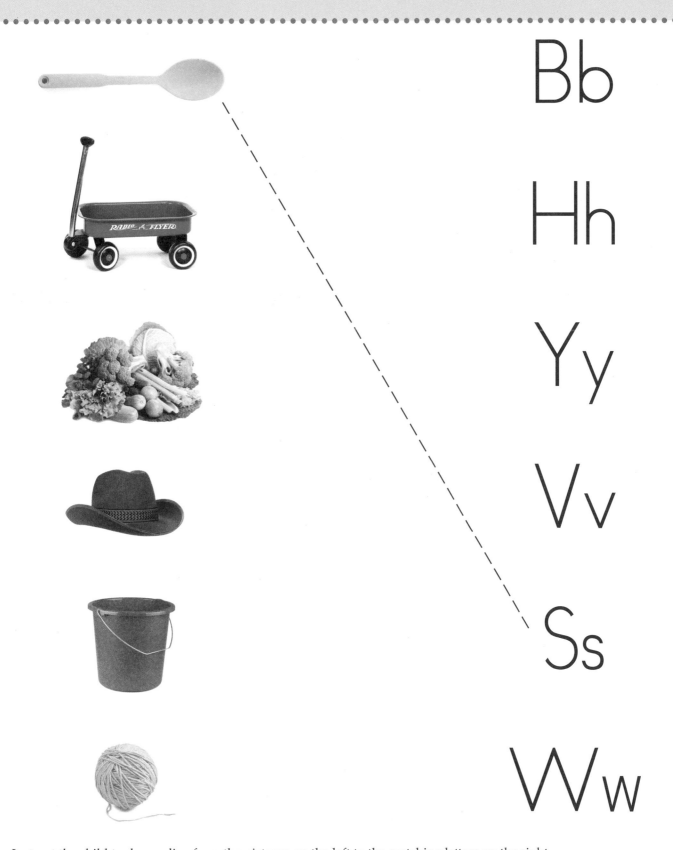

B b

H h

Y y

V v

S s

W w

Instruct the child to draw a line from the pictures on the left to the matching letters on the right.

I can find animals for my zoo.

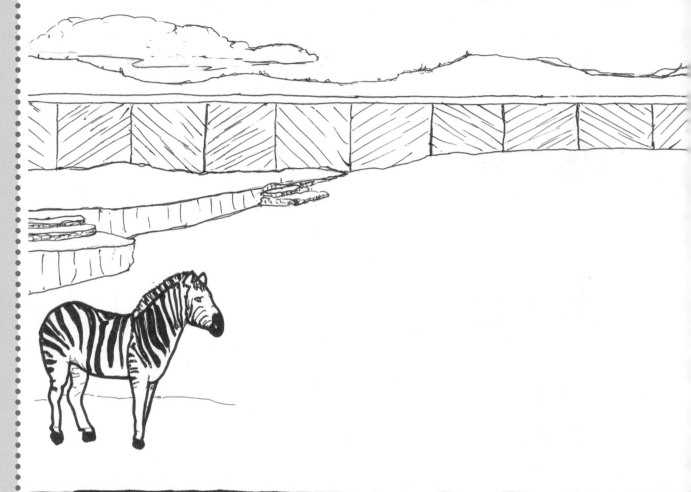

Z z Z z

74

Zacchaeus was little, but he was Jesus' friend, too.

Read the story of Zacchaeus to your child. See Luke 19:1-10 or a children's Bible.

Have the child cut out the zoo animals on page 77. Allow him to paste the animals into his "zoo." As review, ask the child to say the name of each animal and identify which letter and sound each one begins with. (Bear, buh, B; Elephant, eh, E; and so on.)

75

I can match letter sounds.

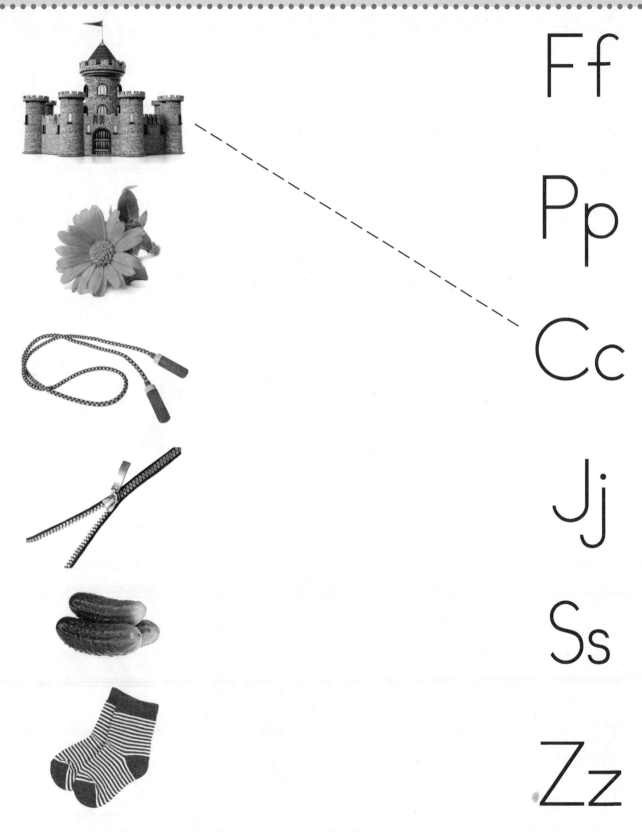

F f

P p

C c

J j

S s

Z z

Instruct the child to draw a line from the pictures on the left to the matching letters on the right.

This page intentionally left blank.

"I Can Find" Letter Guide

Page 79

Frog	Crown	Apple
Mail/Mailbox	Kite	Jesus
Van/Vehicle	Rosary	House/Home
Worm	Pumpkin Pie with Pecans	Dog

Page 81

Violin	Pepperoni Pizza	Green Grapes
Tabernacle	Net	Hearts
Red Rake	Lizard	Blue Bird
Gardening Gloves	Flag	Alligator

Page 83

Kangaroo	Cupcake	Boy with Bat and Ball
Snowman	Ladybug on a Leaf	Duck
Teepee/Tent	Money	Horse
Watermelon	Priest	Fox

Page 85

Turtle/Tortoise	Rainbow	Green Glasses
Watering can	Slide	Jam/Jelly Jar
Nails	Mary	Cow/Calf
Lion	King	Ants

Page 87

Strawberries	Jump rope/Jump	Black Bible/Book
Vase	Nest	Donut

What Is Phonics?

Have you ever approached the sink in an airport restroom only to freeze in confusion as you searched high and low for the water faucet? Perhaps, to the amusement of fellow travelers, you artfully waved your hands around, above, and below the sink in vain hope of locating the latest technological advance in triggering mechanisms. It was only when you stepped back in consternation, accidentally stumbling over a button located on the floor, that water finally gushed forth—if only for a few seconds. Now imagine that, worldwide, each water-dispensing device in sink, tub and shower were unique. Think of the time and frustration involved in learning and memorizing the operation of each individual device that one might encounter over a lifetime. How much time and frustration is saved by familiarity with a few variations of a standardized faucet!

Perhaps this seems an odd way to introduce a comparison between whole-language and phonics approaches to reading. However, the parallel is not such a stretch as it might seem. "Whole-language," or the "look-and-guess" system of reading, requires the reader to memorize thousands of individual words before he can begin to approach literacy. Since he lacks the decoding tools that phonics provides, each word he chances upon is a frustrating unknown. On the other hand, the student of phonics learns word-attack skills that enable him quickly to decipher virtually any word he may encounter.

What is phonics? Simply put, phonics is an approach to reading that begins by teaching letter sounds, then progresses to the blending of those letter sounds to form syllables and words. The English language is comprised of 45 sounds, 21 of which are vowel sounds. Consonant and short vowel sounds are taught first, and can be learned by most children with about three month's instruction. A child who can identify and blend only these sounds already has the word-attack skills to read well in excess of 1,200 words.

In contrast, with the "look-and-guess" or "whole language" approach, the average child memorizes about 300–400 words per year. Since minimal or no instructional time is given to teaching letter sounds or sound blending, the child lacks the skills to decode any word outside his memorized list. By the time the "whole language" student reaches fourth grade, he will be able to identify approximately 1,500 words. Meanwhile, the phonics student will long since have mastered the remaining consonant and vowel blends, gaining the capability of reading more than 24,000 words.

The failure of the "whole language" method extends beyond reading to encompass spelling and nearly every other subject, for virtually all academics are based in some way upon reading. The child who has learned letter sounds and blends has a head start not only in spelling, but also in writing, history, science, math, and religion.

Little Stories for Little Folks
What Makes CHC's Reading Program Unique?

ittle Stories for Little Folks was developed by Nancy Nicholson, who drew on courses in linguistics from her major in Secondary Education—English and comparative studies of phonics programs by Monica Foltzer M.Ed., Edward Fry, Ph.D., Marion Hull, Ph.D., and others. While appreciating the work done by these prominent educators, Nancy Nicholson knew that the average child does not need a course in linguistics in order to learn how to read, and that the average parent does not need (nor have time for) a course in linguistics in order to teach her child how to read. Motivated by this realization, the author set out to develop a phonics program that would:

- maximize ease-of-use for busy parents;
- be interesting and enjoyable for young readers;
- instill a love for our Lord, develop character, and promote Catholic family life.

Nancy Nicholson's approach to phonics is similar to Rosetta Stone's approach to teaching foreign languages. That is, as infants we didn't learn speech by conjugating endless columns of verbs. Rather, we learned verbs within the context of speech. Similarly, instead of requiring the child (and parent) to memorize abstract lists of phonograms and phonics rules, *Little Stories for Little Folks* teaches phonics patterns within the context of word families. Instead of relying on technical terminology ("phoneme," "grapheme," "phonogram"), *Little Stories for Little Folks* utilizes more familiar vocabulary, instructing the child, for example, to be aware of "silent" letters, and letters or sounds that he can "hear."

Teaching phonics-based word families, the author believes, is the most gratifying way for children to discover quickly that there are patterns to words and that they can read a LOT of words even when they are just beginning. Phonics drill can seem so pointless and dry to youngsters that it is almost self-defeating. They want to READ! In *Little Stories for Little Folks*, students are quickly launched into reading interesting, phonics-based short stories, and children discover with the very first story that they can actually read a "whole book"! This early success quickly breeds more success, producing eager readers with excellent word-attack skills.

The testimony of countless homeschooling families confirms the efficacy of Nancy Nicholson's approach. One mother writes: "I LOVE the *Little Stories for Little Folks* phonics program. I had looked at several phonics programs and was reduced to tears due to the complexity/cost of them. Nancy Nicholson's curriculum is easy to read and understand and is affordable!"

Visit www.chcweb.com for more information!

Image Credits:

All images not mentioned below © Catholic Heritage Curricula.

Pg. 21-corn: © matkub2499 / Shutterstock; **pg. 21-drum:** © PHILIPIMAGE / Shutterstock; **pg. 21-egg:** © DragonPhotos / Shutterstock; **pg. 21-ax:** © SolidMaks / Shutterstock; **pg. 21-bear:** © CreativeHQ / Shutterstock; **pg. 31-hotdog:** © JeniFoto / Shutterstock; **pg. 31-igloo:** © Alexey V Smirnov / Shutterstock; **pg. 31-goat:** © yevgeniy11 / Shutterstock; **pg. 31-fish:** © IrinaK / Shutterstock; **pg. 31-bike:** © Gilang Prihardono / Shutterstock; **pg. 45-mouse:** © Alexander Ishchenko / Shutterstock; **pg. 45-nuts:** © George3973 / Shutterstock; **pg. 45-octopus:** © pan demin / Shutterstock; **pg. 45-jello:** © cigdem / Shutterstock; **pg. 45-keys:** © Ian 2010 / Shutterstock; **pg. 45-ladder:** © Jiggo_Putter Studio / Shutterstock; **pg. 51-leaf:** © Ivaylo Ivanov / Shutterstock; **pg. 51-olives:** © Lotus Images / Shutterstock; **pg. 51-pineapple:** © Maks Narodenko / Shutterstock; **pg. 51-hammer:** © Paket / Shutterstock; **pg. 51-monkey:** © Billion Photos / Shutterstock; **pg. 51-quilt:** © dimbar76 / Shutterstock; **pg. 61-pear:** © azure1 / Shutterstock; **pg. 61-queen:** © PysinV / Shutterstock; **pg. 61-saw:** © Tatiana Popova / Shutterstock; **pg. 61-ribbon:** © Dream79 / Shutterstock; **pg. 61-tree:** © Jan Martin Will / Shutterstock; **pg. 61-umbrella:** © adempercem / Shutterstock; **pg. 69-rain:** © YanaKotina / Shutterstock; **pg. 69-vase:** © Mark Brandon / Shutterstock; **pg. 69-watch:** © oksana2010 / Shutterstock; **pg. 69-pumpkin:** © topseller / Shutterstock; **pg. 69-train:** © vvetc1 / Shutterstock; **pg. 69-sun:** © Katsiaryna Chumakova / Shutterstock; **pg. 73-spoon:** © Africa Studio / Shutterstock; **pg. 73-wagon:** © tobkatrina / Shutterstock; **pg. 73-vegetables:** © Aprilphoto / Shutterstock; **pg. 73-hat:** © Seregam / Shutterstock; **pg. 73-bucket:** © Andrey Eremin / Shutterstock; **pg. 73-yarn:** © mama_mia / Shutterstock; **pg. 76-castle:** © cigdem / Shutterstock; **pg. 76-flower:** © D_M / Shutterstock; **pg. 76-jump rope:** © Hurst Photo / Shutterstock; **pg. 76-zipper:** © EtiAmmos / Shutterstock; **pg. 76-pickle:** © domnitsky / Shutterstock; **pg. 76-socks:** © Africa Studio / Shutterstock; **pg. 77-penguin:** © Butterfly Hunter / Shutterstock; **pg. 77-flamingo:** © ILYA AKINSHIN / Shutterstock; **pg. 77-elephant:** © Anan Kaewkhammul / Shutterstock; **pg. 77-lion:** © Eric Isselee / Shutterstock; **pg. 77-kangaroo:** © Eric Isselee / Shutterstock; **pg. 77-gorilla:** © Roman Samokhin / Shutterstock; **pg. 77-tiger:** © Popova Valeriya / Shutterstock; **pg. 77-rhinoceros:** © Mazur Travel / Shutterstock; **pg. 79-frog:** © Chros / Shutterstock; **pg. 79-crown:** © Lawrey / Shutterstock; **pg. 79-apple:** © Artem Kutsenko / Shutterstock; **pg. 79-mail box:** © Ratthaphong Ekariyasap / Shutterstock; **pg. 79-kite:** © Photo Melon / Shutterstock; **pg. 79-Jesus:** © dvande / Shutterstock; **pg. 79-van:** © Rob Wilson / Shutterstock; **pg. 79-rosary:** © Fleckstone / Shutterstock; **pg. 79-house:** © Ratthaphong Ekariyasap / Shutterstock; **pg. 79-worm:** © hsagencia / Shutterstock; **pg. 79-pie:** © Sara Winter / Shutterstock; **pg. 79-dog:** © StudioCAXAP / Shutterstock; **pg. 81-violin:** © AGCuesta / Shutterstock; **pg. 81-pizza:** © bestv / Shutterstock; **pg. 81-net:** © terekhov igor / Shutterstock; **pg. 81-rake:** © Hurst Photo / Shutterstock; **pg. 81-lizard:** © Akugasahagy / Shutterstock; **pg. 81-bird:** © Super Prin / Shutterstock; **pg. 81-gloves:** © Mega Pixel / Shutterstock; **pg. 81-flag:** © Dan Thornberg / Shutterstock; **pg. 81-alligator:** © Chris Shackleford / Shutterstock; **pg. 83-kangaroo:** © Smileus / Shutterstock; **pg. 83-cupcake:** © ami mataraj / Shutterstock; **pg. 83-boy:** © Ljupco Smokovski / Shutterstock; **pg. 83-snowman:** © Madlen / Shutterstock; **pg. 83-leaf:** © Nejron Photo / Shutterstock; **pg. 83-duck:** © Aksenova Natalya / Shutterstock; **pg. 83-teepee:** © Michael Kraus / Shutterstock; **pg. 83-money:** © Robyn Mackenzie / Shutterstock; **pg. 83-horse:** © bagicat / Shutterstock; **pg. 83-watermelon:** © Boonchuay1970 / Shutterstock; **pg. 83-priest:** © Monika Wisniewska / Shutterstock; **pg. 83-fox:** © Eric Isselee / Shutterstock; **pg. 85-turtle:** © fivespots / Shutterstock; **pg. 85-rainbow:** © GreenBelka / Shutterstock; **pg. 85-glasses:** © timquo / Shutterstock; **pg. 85-watering can:** © ILYA AKINSHIN / Shutterstock; **pg. 85-slide:** © Ivan Smuk / Shutterstock; **pg. 85-jam:** © joannawnuk / Shutterstock; **pg. 85-nails:** © Jiri Hera / Shutterstock; **pg. 85-Mary:** © GOLFX / Shutterstock; **pg. 85-cow:** © EtiAmmos / Shutterstock; **pg. 85-lion:** © Eric Isselee / Shutterstock; **pg. 85-king:** © Imgorthand / Shutterstock; **pg. 85-ants:** © Wor Sang Jun / Shutterstock; **pg. 87-strawberries:** © Tim UR / Shutterstock; **pg. 87-boy:** © Africa Studio / Shutterstock; **pg. 87-bible:** © Rose Carson / Shutterstock; **pg. 87-vase:** © Neo Tribbiani / Shutterstock; **pg. 87-nest:** © optimarc / Shutterstock; **pg. 87-donut:** © Hong Vo / Shutterstock.